On The Way To Bethlehem

Advent Dialogues

Richard H. Goodlin

CSS Publishing Company, Inc., Lima, Ohio

ISBN 0-7880-1285-1

These dialogues are dedicated to my wife Marg, because she received meaning and enjoyment from them, and because she provides meaning and enjoyment to me.

Table Of Contents

Introduction

The dialogues that follow were performed at St. Stephen Lutheran Church in Baltimore, Maryland, during the Advent Season, 1995. We call them "dialogues" because they focus on two people, Mary and Joseph.

The dialogues are designed to enhance the Advent Season by reflecting on the persons of Mary and Joseph from the time they hear of the census until the birth of Jesus. Three of the dialogues involve only two characters, Mary and Joseph. One dialogue involves Mary, Joseph, and a neighborhood boy, about eight to ten years old. The dialogue that may be used for Christmas Eve includes a shepherd and his son, along with Mary and Joseph.

Each dialogue may be done as a readers' theater or by memorization. Few props are needed. Costumes are optional. It is suggested that the dialogues be performed after the reading of the Psalm, and just before the lighting of the appropriate candles on an Advent Wreath. The congregation may sing an appropriate Advent hymn while the candles of the Advent wreath are being lit. One hymn suggestion is "Light One Candle to Watch For Messiah," using the stanzas that correspond to the week of Advent.

Dialogue presentations are:

Advent 1:   Hearing The News About The Census
Advent 2:   Preparing For The Journey
Advent 3:   On The Road to Bethlehem
Advent 4:   Approaching Bethlehem
Christmas Eve: The First To Welcome Jesus

Advent 1
Hearing The News About The Census

(Props: small table, chair, bowl, spoon. The small table and chair are set up in the center; the spoon on the table. Mary enters carrying a bowl.)

Mary: Joseph, supper is ready!

(Joseph walks in looking angry and depressed)

Mary: I made some mutton stew for us tonight. How does that sound to you?

Joseph: *(Grumbling)* Fine.

Mary: Just fine? I thought you would be a little more enthused than that!

Joseph: *(Sits on the chair at the table)* I'll like it, don't worry.

Mary: You don't sound like it is fine at all. What is the matter? Didn't Nicodemus like the table you made for them?

Joseph: Nicodemus loved the table!

Mary: Then you should be happy. You spent four weeks making that table. Nicodemus and you have been friends for a long time. You wanted that table to be extra special for him. So if he loved the table, what's the problem?

Joseph: The problem is what Nicodemus told me!

Mary: *(Acting concerned)* What's wrong with Nicodemus?

9

Joseph: Nothing a few dead Romans wouldn't cure!

Mary: What are you talking about?

Joseph: The Romans — those good-for-nothing, stupid, trying-to-control-our-life Romans!

Mary: What did they do now?

Joseph: They want to take a census. It's an excuse to squeeze more taxes out of us.

Mary: Is that all? Taxes are just part of government and life. There is nothing you can do about it, so why waste your time and energy?

Joseph: Because this time they are going too far!

Mary: How so?

Joseph: They are requiring everyone to go to the city in which they were born. That's the most ridiculous thing I ever heard of.

Mary: You mean we have to travel to Bethlehem?

Joseph: You got it!

Mary: Oh dear!

Joseph: I haven't been in Bethlehem for years. We moved up here to Nazareth when I was a boy. I'm not even sure I still have family down there.

Mary: When do we need to be there?

Joseph: Three weeks from today.

Mary: Three weeks! That's not much time. It takes more than a week to get there. That's an eighty-mile trip, and in my condition, it will probably take longer.

Joseph: In your condition, you shouldn't even try to make the trip.

Mary: So who ever said the Romans had compassion?

Joseph: This really ticks me off. Why make people go to their place of birth when they don't live there any more? Who cares where you live — taxes are taxes. They take the money and use it for their good, not ours.

Mary: Maybe that's the way God wants it. After all, this is God's child, the one sent by God. Remember, the angel told me that God would make him a king like his ancestor David. And Bethlehem is the city of King David.

Joseph: People will have a hard time believing that the son of a carpenter is a king. Even if he grows up and develops a following, the Romans will make sure he is dead before he gets to be king.

Mary: Joseph, you have always been a man of great faith. Trust in God. If this truly is God's child that I carry, God will make sure no harm comes to him. Come on, eat your supper. We'll worry about this census and trip to Bethlehem later.

Joseph: Okay, maybe a good meal will calm me down.

Advent 2
Preparing For The Journey

(Props: a duffle bag, some clothes, some food, water bottle. Joseph is working with the props as if in the last stages of packing. The boy Lazarus enters to begin.)

Lazarus: Hi, Mr. Joe.

Joseph: Hi, Lazarus. How are you today?

Lazarus: I'm fine. It looks like you are planning to travel.

Joseph: *(Not happy with the idea)* Yes, Miss Mary and I have to go to Bethlehem.

Lazarus: What's down in Bethlehem?

Joseph: That's where I was born. The Romans are making us travel there to conduct a census.

Lazarus: Oh, yes. I overheard my dad and mom talking about that. We were all born here in Nazareth, so we can stay here, but they said some people would have to make long trips. I guess you are one of them.

Joseph: Unfortunately, that's right.

Lazarus: How long will you be gone?

Joseph: It might be a month or more. Miss Mary is in no condition to travel fast, and I am not sure what all has to be done to fulfill this census. Down and back will take at least twenty days of travel.

Mary: *(Coming on to the scene as if coming from inside the house)* Hi, Lazarus.

Lazarus: Hi, Miss Mary. Mr. Joe was just telling me about you having to travel to Bethlehem for the census.

Mary: Yes, it is certainly not something we are looking forward to. That's a long, hard trip.

Lazarus: I hope nothing happens to your baby on the way.

Mary: I'm not worried. This is a child of God, so I am confident that God will take care of him.

Lazarus: Well, I gotta run. *(Leaves the scene)*

Mary: Have a good day, Lazarus. *(To Joseph)* Lazarus is a really nice boy. I wonder if our son will be as nice.

Joseph: If he is God's child, he'd better be.

Mary: Do we have everything for the trip?

Joseph: I think so. We have water bottles. Some extra clothes. Some food. It is hard to figure out just what to take. We'll have to get food along the way from wild fig trees and olive trees, maybe a kind farmer or two. We can't afford to buy all the food we need for the trip, let alone carry it all. And I have no idea where we will be sleeping!

Mary: Relax, Joseph. Everything will be fine. Maybe we will come across some other people on their way to Bethlehem, or some other town.

Joseph: Keep telling me that — I am not looking forward to this trip. The Romans give us three weeks notice. I am backed up on the furniture I have promised people I would make for them. And you are going to give birth to a baby any day now. How can you not be worried and upset!

Mary: Maybe it's just the good feeling I have about this child I am carrying. Every child is special to God, but this one is extra special. Even before he is born, he is bringing me peace and joy.

Joseph: You are amazing, Mary. You have always been so calm in troubled times. I hope nothing ever happens to shake that.

Mary: I hope so too. *(Pause)* However, I am a bit worried. *(Hesitatingly)* I know that God has great plans for this child, but I also know that change never comes easily. I am sure that there will be some people who will not be happy with the changes he brings.

Joseph: That's a long way off. He has to be born and grow up first. We may both be dead by the time he comes to power and makes the changes.

Mary: That would be okay with me. I'm most fearful of having to watch my son die.

Joseph: And these Romans are good at killing people to stop them from coming to power. They seem to especially delight in crucifixions.

Mary: Oh, don't say that! Just thinking of the possibility of my son being crucified sends chills up my spine!

Joseph: You're right. Enough of this morbid talk. Our child will bring much more joy and peace and goodwill than heartache. God will see to that.

Advent 3
On The Road To Bethlehem

(Props: walking stick, duffle bag from Advent 2. Mary and Joseph are walking from one side of stage/chancel to the other as they begin to talk.)

Joseph: Do you need to rest, Mary?

Mary: No, I'm doing fine, Joseph. So far, the journey hasn't been too bad.

Joseph: We've been making better time than I thought we would. I figure we can make Jerusalem in about three more days, and Bethlehem is only a day and a half journey from there.

Mary: That sounds good to me. I would rather get to Bethlehem early than be rushed.

Joseph: You know, I've never been to Jerusalem. I've always wanted to go there. What would you think about spending a few days there and seeing the sights?

(Mary grabs her stomach and utters a painful groan. At center stage, she and Joseph stop walking and continue conversation.)

Joseph: What's the matter?

Mary: Nothing. I think it was just the baby kicking.

Joseph: You doubled up like it was much more than just a baby kicking.

Mary: No, I think it was just a powerful kick.

Joseph: Are you sure? This is no time to take chances. We can skip Jerusalem if you want.

Mary: No, it wouldn't be right to skip Jerusalem. Jerusalem is an important place. We can stop there if you want.

Joseph: It shouldn't be too crowded. It is not Passover when everyone travels to Jerusalem and the city gets overcrowded.

Mary: I remember my cousin telling me about riots in Jerusalem during Passover. Some of the nicest people turn vicious.

Joseph: The Romans probably incited them to riot just so they could arrest and torture some Jews.

Mary: Joseph, how can you say that!

Joseph: I'm still angry at having to make this trip. As far as I'm concerned, the less we have to deal with the Romans the better.

Mary: Take it easy, Joseph. I'm sure there are some Romans who are decent people. Most of them are just doing their jobs.

Joseph: And I'm just doing my job as a good Jew by complaining about them.

Mary: So — what do you want to see in Jerusalem?

Joseph: The Temple.

Mary: The Temple certainly is the most important place.

Joseph: I've heard great stories about the Temple and all its beauty. They say that just to stand in the middle of the Temple makes you feel like you are in the presence of God.

Mary: With all the violence and uncertainty of today, we need God to be present with us in a very real way.

Joseph: Maybe hearing the temple priests will help us feel the presence of God. After all, the temple priests are the most holy of men.

Mary: *(Grabs stomach and again groans in pain)* There goes that kick again!

Joseph: Are you sure you are all right? I worry about you.

Mary: I'm fine. I think it's the baby that doesn't want to go to Jerusalem.

Joseph: Why wouldn't a child of God want to go to Jerusalem?

Mary: Maybe the people there aren't as friendly as the people in Galilee.

Joseph: Maybe now is not the time to go to Jerusalem. That baby may be coming sooner than we think. It's probably more important for us to get to Bethlehem. Visiting Jerusalem can wait.

Mary: I'm sure that our child will get to Jerusalem sometime in his life.

(Mary and Joseph continue their walking)

Advent 4
Approaching Bethlehem

(Props: Duffle bag, walking stick. Mary and Joseph are walking slowly across the front of the chancel/stage.)

Mary: Joseph ...

Joseph: Yes, Mary.

Mary: How much further do we have to go?

Joseph: Why? Is something wrong?

Mary: No, I was just wondering. *(Pause)* Joseph ...

Joseph: Yes, Mary?

Mary: Have you had any experience in delivering babies?

Joseph: No.

Mary: I think you're going to get some experience in delivering babies.

Joseph: You mean it's time?

Mary: I'm not sure.

Joseph: What do you mean, you're not sure?

Mary: Well, I never had a baby before.

Joseph: Oh, this is just great. Here we are in the middle of nowhere, and neither one of us with any experience in delivering a baby. I was hoping we would get to Bethlehem before the baby came, so that we could get some help.

Mary: Can we rest a while?

Joseph: Sure. Here, sit down on this rock. *(A chair or chancel step could serve as a rock)*

Mary: How much further do we have to go?

Joseph: I figured we would get there tomorrow.

Mary: Do you think we could make it there today?

Joseph: Possibly, but we would have to travel into the night. I don't think we could make it before nightfall. How soon do you think you will deliver the baby?

Mary: I don't know. Some women have told me they had labor pains for days. Others said it was over in a matter of minutes.

Joseph: I wish we could have stayed with that group that was going to Jericho. They were friendly and wanted to be helpful.

Mary: A lot friendlier than the people we met in Jerusalem.

Joseph: That's for sure. If they had been friendlier in Jerusalem, I would turn back.

Mary: We shouldn't worry. We'll make it to Bethlehem before this baby is born. This baby is destined to be born in Bethlehem.

Joseph: I hope you are right. It would be better for us to get to Bethlehem before the baby is born. A birth is already too risky. And negotiating a successful birth here in the middle of nowhere is not my thing. I'm a carpenter, not a midwife.

Mary: Have faith, Joseph. Remember, this is God's child. Nothing will happen to him.

Joseph: Keep reminding me of that.

Mary: Joseph ...

Joseph: Don't tell me — It is getting painful, isn't it? Do you want to stop here? You are more important than any Roman census!

Mary: I'd rather see if we could make it to Bethlehem, even if it means traveling far into the night. I think this baby is anxious to be born, but I believe God wants him to be born in Bethlehem. I'll be all right.

Joseph: Well, they did say we could make it from Jerusalem to Bethlehem in one day if we pushed it. I hope they are right. Are you ready?

Mary: Yes, let's go. We must make it to Bethlehem today.

(Mary and Joseph get up and continue to walk)

Christmas Eve
The First To Welcome Jesus

(Mary and Joseph with manger are toward one side of stage. Mary sitting, Joseph standing. Shepherd (Dad) and son enter from opposite side of stage/chancel and begin conversation.)

Son: Dad ...

Dad: Yes, son.

Son: Do you really think the angels were right?

Dad: I don't know. I only know that never in my thirty years of shepherding have I seen anything like what we saw tonight!

Son: I was scared!

Dad: So was I!

Son: Dad, why would a baby be in a manger?

Dad: I don't know. Maybe because the city is so overcrowded with people here for the census, there just wasn't any other place for them to find shelter.

Son: There are lots of mangers around Bethlehem. How are we going to know which one to go to?

Dad: We just have to keep looking until we find it, or until we conclude that the angels were wrong.

Son: Dad, if the baby is in a manger, would the animals try to eat it?

Dad: *(Half laughing)* No, son. I'm sure that the mother and father are close by protecting it. And besides that, if this is truly the Savior as the angels said, God is protecting him.

Son: What are we going to say when we get there?

Dad: Well, usually if it is a baby boy, we say he looks just like his father.

Son: But what if he doesn't look like his father?

Dad: It doesn't matter. You say that anyway. It makes the father feel good.

Son: Did they say that about me when I was born?

Dad: Oh, yes, and it made me very happy.

Son: Do you think I will really grow up to look like you?

Dad: There will probably be some resemblance, but you won't look exactly like me.

Son: What about this baby? Will he grow up to look like his father?

Dad: I imagine that when he grows up, people will know who his father is by what he says, and by the way he acts.

Son: *(Pointing to where Mary and Joseph are)* Look, Dad, there is a manger over there, and there are two people by it.

Dad: Well, let's go over and see if this is the one we have been looking for.

(Shepherd and son go over to Mary and Joseph)

Dad: Congratulations on the birth of your son!

Joseph: Thank you.

Dad: What is his name?

Joseph: Jesus.

Dad: You look like you have just finished traveling a long way to get here.

Joseph: We came from Nazareth, and just arrived a couple of hours ago.

Dad: *(Looking at Mary)* That must have been a hard trip for you!

Mary: I was confident we would make it.

Dad: This is an extra hardship you don't need — a long journey, and then having to find shelter with the animals.

Joseph: The inn is full. I couldn't even bribe a room. But the innkeeper was kind enough to let us use this shelter reserved for the animals.

Mary: It reminds me that God cares for all of us, even we who cannot afford a place to stay.

Dad: We were visited by angels tonight as we guarded our sheep. They told us to come to Bethlehem, because our savior was born. Is this the savior we are looking for?

Mary: Yes, I believe so. I was visited by an angel, even before I was with child. The angel told me that I would give birth to God's child.

Joseph: Visits from angels, making a long trip with a baby due any day, finding shelter in an overcrowded town — there is no doubt in my mind that God is in this child. He must be the Savior.

Son: *(Speaking to Joseph)* Sir, I think the baby looks just like his father.

Joseph: *(Smiling broadly and after short pause)* That makes me very happy! Thanks be to God!

Son: *(Looking at congregation)* Everyone should say, "Thanks be to God!"

(Actors lead congregation in saying,"Thanks be to God!")

www.ingramcontent.com/pod-product-compliance
Lightning Source LLC
Chambersburg PA
CBHW071810020426
42331CB00008B/2454